Silver Burdett Ginn Science
DISCOVERYWORKS

 HOUGHTON MIFFLIN

Boston • Atlanta • Dallas • Denver • Geneva, Illinois • Palo Alto • Princeton

Authors

William Badders
Science Resource Teacher
Cleveland Public Schools
Cleveland, OH

Lowell J. Bethel
Professor of Science Education
The University of Texas at Austin
Austin, TX

Victoria Fu
Professor of Child Development
Virginia Polytechnic Institute and
State University
Blacksburg, VA

Donald Peck
Director, Center for Elementary Science
Fairleigh Dickinson University
Madison, NJ

Carolyn Sumners
Director of Astronomy and Physics
Houston Museum of Natural Science
Houston, TX

Catherine Valentino
Senior Vice President for
Curriculum Development
Voyager Expanded Learning
West Kingston, RI

Consulting Author

R. Mike Mullane
Astronaut, retired
Albuquerque, NM

Contributing Writers

Wendy Pfeffer
Jeanne Gleason

Credits and acknowledgements appear on page H29,
which constitutes an extension of this copyright page.

CONTENTS

UNIT A

INTERACTIONS OF LIVING THINGS

Themes: Constancy and Change; Models

Sorting **Objects**

WHAT YOU NEED

empty paper bag

bag of woodland objects

hand lens

Science Notebook

1. Collect objects from the schoolyard in a bag.

2. Sort the objects into two groups: living and once-living in one group and nonliving in another group. List the objects in each group.

3. Repeat step 2, using woodland objects.

4. Use a hand lens to look at the groups of objects. Compare woodland objects with schoolyard objects.

Think! How did you decide which objects to put in each group?

Living and Nonliving Things

Imagine being in this woodland. How might you classify the things around you? You could classify them as living, once-living, or nonliving things.

A **living thing** needs food, water, and air. It can grow. A living thing can also make new living things. The trees and other plants are living things.

Once-living things are not living now. They were living in the past. What things in the picture were once living? Dead leaves, the logs of the bridge, and broken twigs are once-living things.

Nonliving things have never needed food, water, or air. They have not grown. They have not made new living things. Rocks are nonliving things.

Making a
Terrarium

WHAT YOU NEED

goggles

container and lid with air holes

gravel

soil

watering can with water

plants

living animals

Science Notebook

1. Spread gravel in the container. Cover the gravel with soil.

2. Add water to the soil.

3. Put the plants into the soil.

4. Add some animals. Give them food and water.

5. Cover your terrarium. Talk about how to care for it. Record your plan.

Think! How do living things in the terrarium get what they need?

Living Things Have Needs

A **habitat** is the home of a living thing. In a habitat, plants and animals get what they need to live.

The first picture shows a desert habitat. There is food, air, and light for the living things. There is not much water. Desert plants and animals can live where there is little water.

The second picture shows a seacoast habitat. It also has food, air, and light. The seacoast has a lot of water. It is salty water. Some plants and animals make their homes in the sea. They need salty water to live.

The picture shows colorful sea stars. A sea star is an animal that eats other animals. The sea star gets what it needs from its seacoast habitat.

Observing Roots

tray with seedlings
on a paper towel

hand lens

tweezers

Science Notebook

1. Use a hand lens to look at seedlings.
Talk about what the roots look like.
Draw what you see.

INTERACTIONS OF LIVING THINGS

2. Carefully turn the paper towel upside down and shake gently. Record what happens.

3. Gently try to pull a seedling off the towel. Watch the roots closely while you do this. Record what happens.

Think! How do roots help a plant to survive?

prickly pear cactus

All About Plants

What parts do both of these plants have? They both have roots. **Roots** help hold each plant in the soil. Roots also take in water and minerals from the soil.

Both plants have stems. **Stems** carry water and food to other parts of the plant. The stem in a cactus also makes food and stores water.

dandelion

Leaves make food for a plant. Different plants have different kinds of leaves. The dandelion has broad, flat leaves. The cactus has tiny, sharp leaves called **spines.** Spines help protect the cactus by keeping animals from eating it. Plants lose less water from spines than from broad, flat leaves. Turn the page to see these parts labeled.

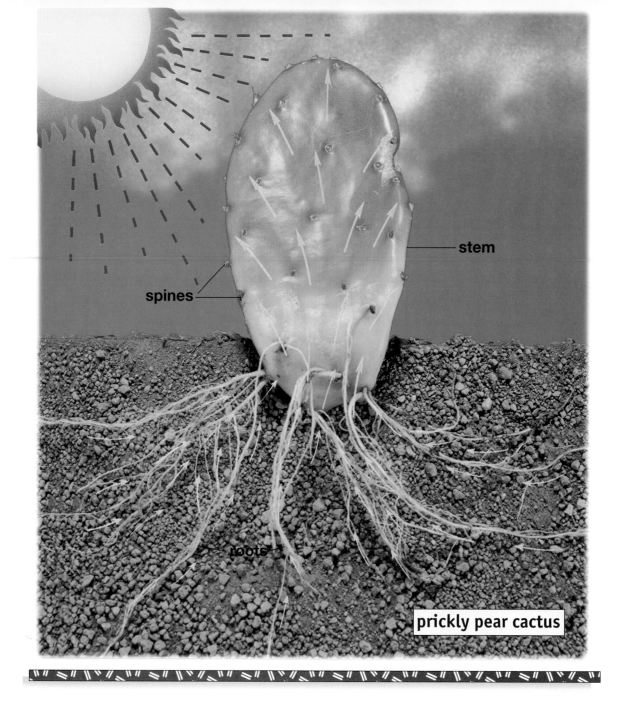

spines

stem

roots

prickly pear cactus

How does a plant get what it needs to live? Point to the roots, stem, and spines of the cactus. Follow the blue arrows up from the roots. The arrows show how water moves through a cactus.

Look at the dandelion. Water and minerals move from the roots to the stems to the leaves. This is how the plants get what they need.

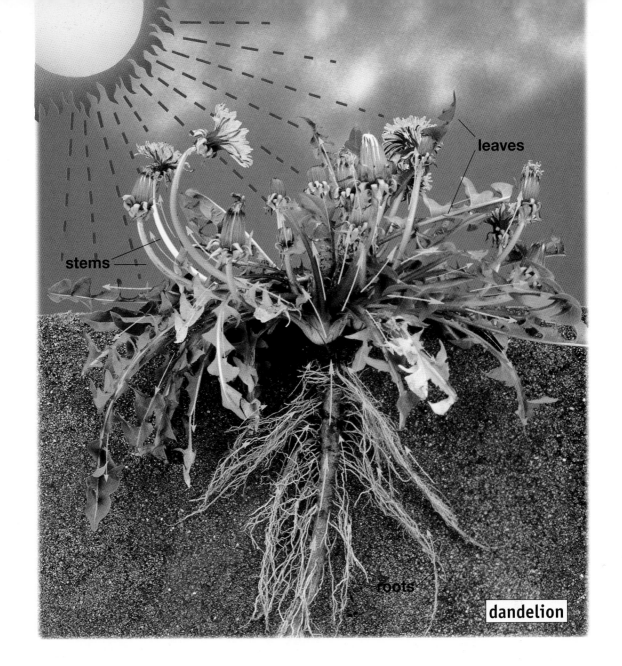

leaves

stems

roots

dandelion

The roots of these plants are different. The cactus lives in the desert. Its roots stay near the top of the soil. This helps them take in water quickly when rain falls.

Plants need more than food, water, and air to live. They also need light. The plants in the picture are getting light from the sun. Plants use sunlight to help them make food.

Finding
Shelter

WHAT YOU NEED

hand lens

sow bugs

terrarium

wood with bark

plant sprayer with water

Science Notebook

1. Use a hand lens to look at a sow bug.
Draw what you see.

2. Predict where sow bugs will go when you put them in a terrarium. Put them in and record what happens.

3. Spray the wood with water. Put the wood in the terrarium.

4. Move the sow bug to a dry spot in the terrarium. Record what the sow bug does. Talk about why you think it does this.

Think! How does a sow bug use the terrarium to meet its needs?

Meeting Needs

A swamp is a habitat. Many plants and animals live in a swamp. Water covers the land in a swamp most of the time.

Look at the picture. You can see water, trees, grasses, and an alligator. Birds also live in swamps. How is a swamp different from a desert or a woodland?

INTERACTIONS OF LIVING THINGS

Things that plants and animals use to live are called **resources.** The alligator uses living things in the swamp for food. It eats frogs, birds, and other animals.

The alligator also uses nonliving things to live. These things include air, light, and water. Look again at the picture. What other things in the swamp might an animal use to live?

Building an
Ant Farm

WHAT YOU NEED

goggles

ant farm kit

measuring cup with water

ants

Science Notebook

1. Follow the directions in the kit. Fill the ant farm with sand.

2. Add water.

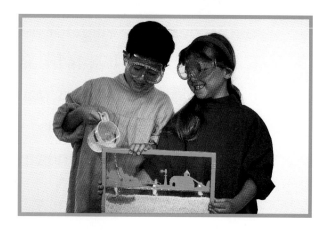

3. Push the cotton stoppers down into the sand. Add food.

4. Add ants. Observe the ants and record what you see.

Think! How do ants use the ant farm?

robin

mole

ants and eggs

earthworm

rabbit

Underground Homes

All animals need a shelter. A **shelter** is a place
where an animal can rest and be safe. It protects the
animal from heat and cold. It is a place to store food. It
is also a place to take care of young.

Shelters can be made with living and nonliving
things. Shelters can be in many places.

chipmunk

Look at the picture. Some of the animals make their homes underground. The mother rabbit puts grass in her shelter. She makes a soft nest for her young.

The chipmunk stores acorns in its shelter. The ants lay their eggs in tunnels. The earthworms find food in the soil. All these animals made their homes by digging into the soil.

Eating
Like a Bird

WHAT YOU NEED

goggles

tweezers

slotted spoon

uncooked rice
on a log

foam peanuts in
a container of water

Science Notebook

1. Pretend each tool is a bird's mouth and the peanuts and rice are bird food.

2. Use each tool to pick up one piece of rice.

3. Use each tool to pick up some foam peanuts.

4. Which mouth worked better to pick up each kind of food? Record your findings.

Think! Why was one type of mouth better for picking up some kinds of foods?

Fish in the water

Bugs on a log

toco toucan

downy woodpecker

Getting Food

Animals have body parts that help them live. A
beak is a mouth part that helps a bird get food.

Some birds have beaks that are used to pick up tiny
things like seeds or nuts. The toucan carries eggs in its
beak. The woodpecker uses its beak to drill through
nuts and bark to get food.

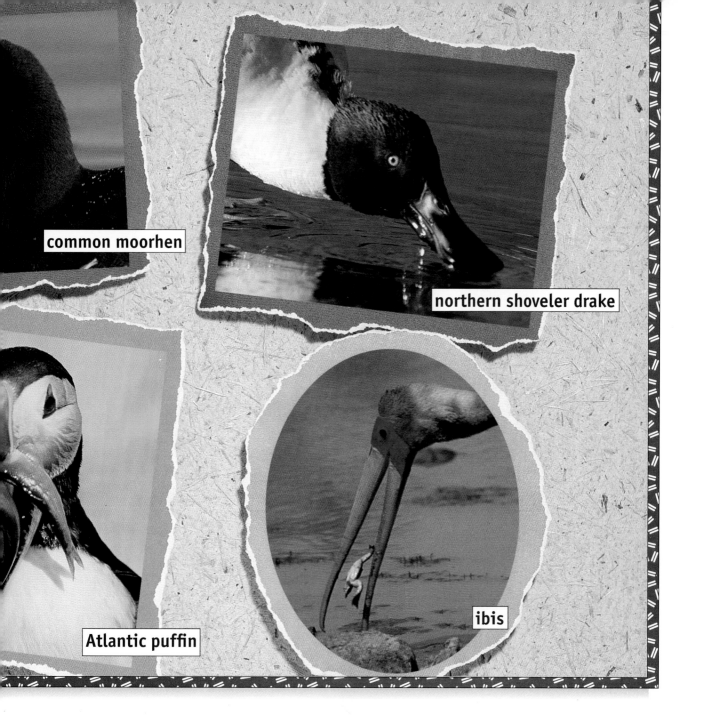

common moorhen

northern shoveler drake

Atlantic puffin

ibis

The long beak of the ibis is used to spear fish or frogs in shallow water. The puffin's beak is good for gobbling up many small fish.

Some birds have scooping beaks that are also called bills. The moorhen and the drake are birds that live in water. They eat plants. They use their bills to scoop plants out of the water.

Building a
Beaver Dam

WHAT YOU NEED

goggles

large tray

soil

twigs

clay

books

watering can with water

Science Notebook

1. Cover the bottom of a tray with soil. Make a riverbed down the center with your fingers.

2. Build a dam by twisting twigs together. Pack any holes in the dam with clay. Place the dam across the riverbed.

3. Place some books under one end of the tray.

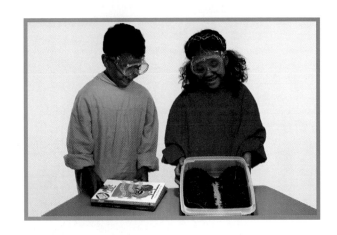

4. Predict what will happen when you pour water down the riverbed. Pour water slowly and record what you see.

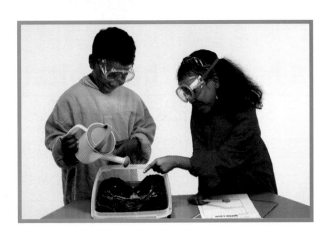

Think! Why does a beaver build a dam?

Changing the Habitat

Some animals make changes to the place in which they live. A beaver is one such animal. It uses its teeth to cut down trees. Look at the tree that the beaver is cutting. The cut tree will fall in the river. This is the beginning of a beaver dam. The beaver dam will cross the riverbed from one side to the other.

The three small photos show a beaver at work. The beaver uses its sharp teeth to cut down trees. As it swims, it carries twigs in its mouth. It uses its legs, feet, and tail to swim. Its paddle-shaped tail helps it pack twigs, stones, and mud around the trees.

Turn the page. See how the woodland looks after the beaver builds its dam.

The beaver has built the dam. A pond has formed behind it. The pond is a place of still water. Here the beaver builds its shelter.

The beaver's shelter is called a **lodge.** It is made of the same things the beaver used for the dam—trees, twigs, mud, and stones. A beaver stays warm, stores food, and raises its young in a lodge.

The beaver changes the woodland in many ways. When the beaver cuts down trees, animals that lived in those trees lose their homes. Animals that eat parts of trees, such as fruit or leaves, lose their food.

The pond that forms behind the dam floods some of the land. Animals that lived on that land need to find new homes.

Washing Away the Land

WHAT YOU NEED

goggles

pan with soil in it

books

large towel

watering can with water

pan with soil and plants in it

Science Notebook

1. Make a hill by putting books under one end of a pan with soil in it.

2. Place a towel under the lower end of the pan. Pour water down the hill. Record what happens.

3. Put books under one end of a pan with plants in it. Predict what you think will happen when you pour water down this hill.

4. Repeat step 2, using the pan with the plants in it.

Think! How do plants affect the flow of water down a hill?

More Changes

People can change an area. Natural forces can also change an area. Changes can be both helpful and harmful. Look at the picture. In what ways are people helping and harming this area?

Planting trees and picking up trash are helpful. Building a road or a house can harm an area.

INTERACTIONS OF LIVING THINGS

Cutting down trees can cause erosion. **Erosion** is the washing away of land. The roots of trees can help stop erosion. Roots hold soil in place.

Forest fires can be helpful or harmful. They are helpful when they clear away twigs, leaves, and dead trees. Forest fires are harmful when they kill living things.

Making a
Desert Garden

goggles

bowl

gravel

mixture of sand and potting soil

spoon

small cactuses

aloe

watering can with water

hand lens

Science Notebook

1. Put gravel in the bottom of the bowl. Spread soil over the gravel.

2. Make holes in the soil. Put the plants into the holes. Water the plants just a little.

3. Break off a small piece of aloe. Use a hand lens to look at the inside of the plant. Record what you see.

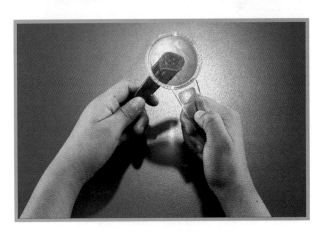

4. Talk about how to care for your desert garden. Record your plan.

Think! What would happen to these plants if you watered them too much?

Living in the Desert

A desert is a place that gets very little rain. There are many kinds of living things in this desert. What kinds of living things do you see?

Many of the plants in this picture are cactuses. Like other plants, they are green and have stems and roots. How are cactuses different from other plants?

INTERACTIONS OF LIVING THINGS

Desert plants and animals need the same things as other plants and animals. They need food, water, air, and light.

Desert plants and animals can live where the days are very hot and the nights are cold. They can also live with very little water. What plants and animals could not stay alive in the desert?

Comparing Woodland and Desert Plants

WHAT YOU NEED

woodland terrarium

desert garden

hand lens

Science Notebook

1. Use a hand lens to look at the plants and soil in the woodland terrarium and the desert garden. Record how they are alike and different.

2. Talk about what would happen to a woodland plant if you put it in the desert garden.

3. Talk about what would happen to a desert plant if you put it in a woodland environment.

Think! If all plants need water, how can some plants live where it is dry?

Some Other Habitats

These two animals live in different places. The polar bear lives where it is cold and snowy. The flamingo lives where it is warm and wet.

What helps a polar bear live in the Arctic? It has thick fur that helps keep it warm. Its fur is white. This color helps a polar bear hide on ice and snow.

What helps a flamingo live in wet places? Its long legs help it wade in water to find food. Its bill helps it scoop food out of the water. This bird also uses its bill to scoop mud as it builds a nest.

Polar bears and flamingos cannot live in the desert. A desert would be too warm and dry for a polar bear. It would be too dry for a flamingo.

Word Power

A. Match the words with a picture.
living thing   once-living thing   nonliving thing

a.   b.   c.

B. Use these words to fill in the blanks.

stems	roots	leaves	resources
beaks	lodge	erosion	shelter

1. The underground parts of plants are _____.

2. Body parts that help birds get food are _____.

3. Things that plants and animals use to live
are _____.

4. The washing away of soil is _____.

5. The parts of a plant that carry food and water to
other parts are the _____.

6. For most plants, food is made in the _____.

7. A beaver builds a home called a _____.

8. A place where an animal can rest and raise young
is a _____.

Using Science Ideas

How many living things can you find in this woodland habitat? List them.

Solving Science Problems

1. Why do living things need food, water, air, and light?

2. Why can't a polar bear live in the desert?

3. Make a chart like the one shown. Add more living things. Then complete your chart.

Living Thing	Habitat	Special Features
polar bear	Arctic	thick fur

UNIT B

LIGHT AND COLOR

Theme: Systems

Finding
Light Sources

WHAT YOU NEED

crayons

Science Notebook

---

1. Draw objects that give off light.

2. Talk about which objects are made by people. Color those objects.

3. Make a class list of objects that give off light. Divide your list into two parts: (1) natural light and (2) light made by people.

Think! Which object that gives off light is the most important? Tell why you think so.

Looking for Light

Many things in this picture give off **light.** Some are made by people. Others are natural. Which things that give off light are natural? The stars in the sky are natural things that give off light. The burning logs are also natural things that give off light. Our most important source of light is not in this picture.

The sun is our most important source of light. It makes life on the earth possible. Other natural things that give off light are lightning and fireflies.

Electric bulbs give off light and are made by people. Oil lamps and gaslights also give off light. They too are made by people. What other things that give off light are made by people?

Looking at Objects
With and Without Light

WHAT YOU NEED

crayons

large index card

paper grocery bag

tape

flashlight

Science Notebook

1. Draw a picture, but don't let anyone see it. Tape your picture to the bottom of the inside of a paper bag.

2. Darken the room. Ask someone to look inside the bag and tell about your picture.

3. Keep the room dark. Repeat step 2, shining a flashlight into the bag.

4. Make the room light again. Ask someone to look inside the bag and tell about your picture.

Think! When were you best able to see the picture? Tell why.

Lighting Up the Night

Some animals, such as owls and cats, can see well when there is very little light. People need more light to see well.

In the picture above, the room is dark. The boy can't see clearly. Things look different to him than they really are. He thinks animals are in the room.

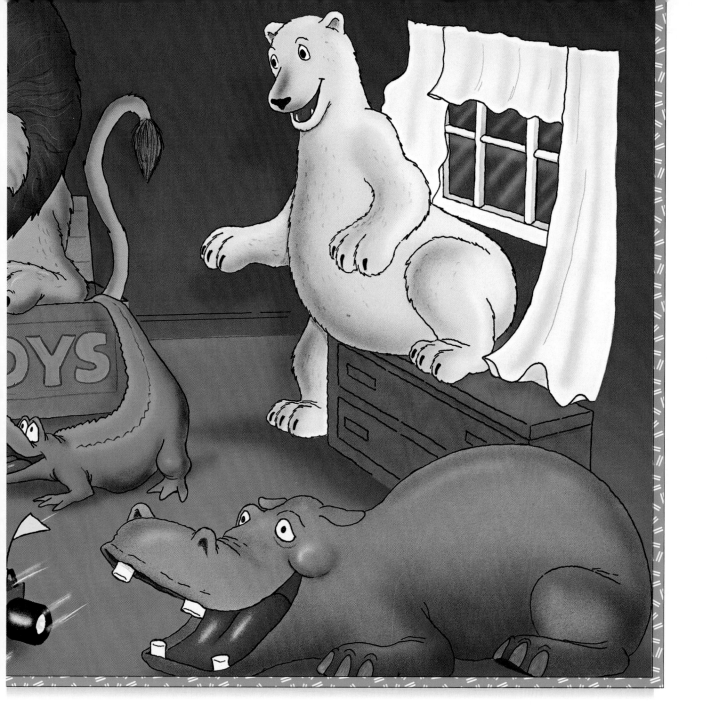

If you look outdoors in the dark, you might imagine
you see something that really isn't there. At night, a
few trees might look like a jungle. A fire hydrant might
look like a monkey.

When you look outdoors during the day, things look
different. Turn the page to see what the boy's room
looks like in the light.

Light helps the boy see what's really there. There are no animals in the room.

When do you use light? You might use a lamp to help you read at night. You might use a flashlight to brighten a dark path. You might use a nightlight to light up a hallway at night.

The moon can help you see at night. It does not give off its own light. The moon **reflects** sunlight. That means sunlight hits the moon and bounces off it.

Light can help keep people safe. Streetlights brighten the sidewalks for people who are walking. Bike reflectors help drivers see riders at night.

Exploring Heat From the Sun

WHAT YOU NEED

2 ice cubes the same size

2 pieces of black cloth

2 aluminum pie plates

stopwatch

Science Notebook

1. Predict whether an ice cube will melt faster in the sun or in the shade. Record your prediction.

2. Wrap each cube in cloth. Place each one in its own pie plate. Put one in the sun and one in the shade.

LIGHT AND COLOR

3. Wait 5 minutes. Check both ice cubes and record what you see.

4. Rewrap the ice cubes and repeat step 3.

Think! Which ice cube melted faster? Tell why.

Light and Heat

Imagine sitting by a campfire like the one in the picture. How would you feel? You would feel warm. The fire provides both light and **heat.** What other objects in the picture give off light and heat? The flashlight, the lantern, and the stars all give off light and heat. Some objects give off more light and heat than others.

The closer you are to a light source, the more heat you feel. Most stars are very far away. You do not feel their heat. One star is close enough for you to feel its heat. That star is the sun. The sun lights and heats the earth's air, land, and water.

Which people in the picture feel the most heat from the campfire? Which people feel the least?

Observing
a Beam of Light

WHAT YOU NEED

line cards A–D    flashlight   Science Notebook

1. Place card A on your desk. Darken the room.

2. Aim a flashlight along the line on card A. Try to make the beam of light follow the line. Record what you see.

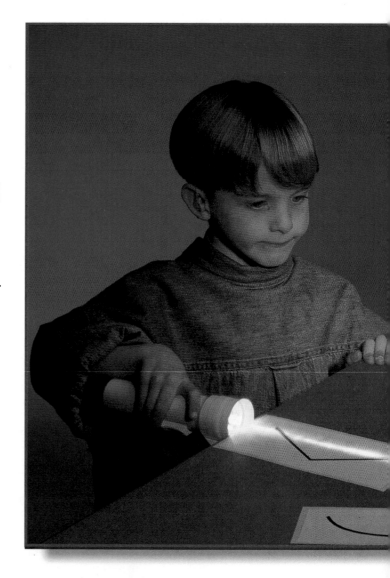

3. Repeat step 2 for the other line cards. Record what you see.

Think! What did you learn about how a beam of light travels?

Beams of Light

What fun it is to play hide-and-seek! In this game, the person who is "it" must shine a flashlight on each child. Think about how light travels. Where might you hide so you won't get caught? You might hide behind a tree. The tree would block the **beam** of light. Why does the tree block the light?

Light travels in **straight** lines. That's why the tree blocks the beam of light. Light does not curve around an object, such as a tree or a play car.

How does light get from an electric light bulb to a book? Beams of light travel out from the bulb in all directions. Each beam travels in a straight line. Some beams shine on the pages of the book.

Observing Light As It Strikes Objects

WHAT YOU NEED

flashlight

cup of water

cup of milky water

waxed paper

tissue paper

newspaper

foil

construction paper

clear plastic wrap

mirror

Science Notebook

1. Predict whether all light, some light, or no light will pass through the objects. Record your predictions.

2. Darken the room. Shine a flashlight through a cup of clear water. Record what happens to the light.

3. Try to shine light through the other objects. Record what happens.

4. Compare your predictions with your observations.

Think! How are the objects that do not let light pass through them alike?

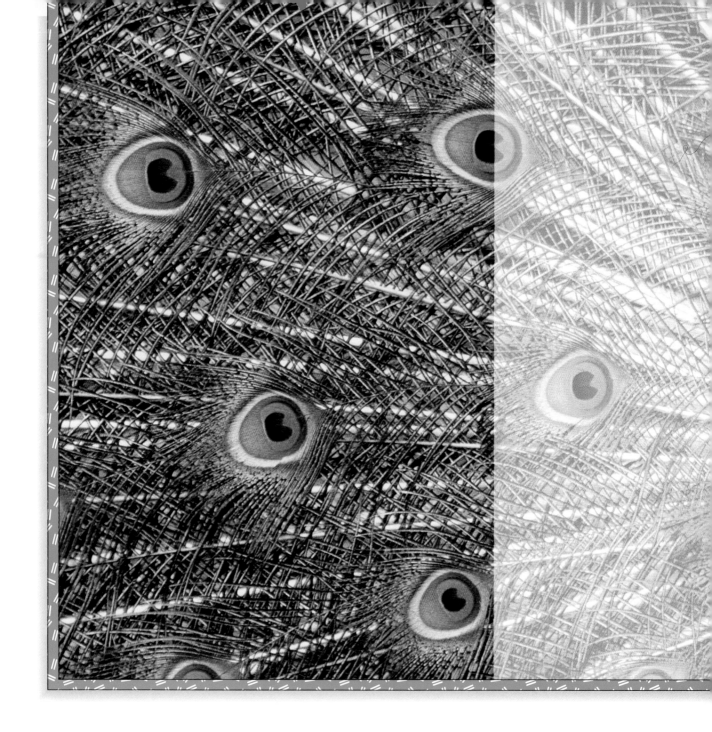

Can You See the Light?

Light passes through some objects. Those objects are **transparent.** Some objects let a little light through. They are **translucent.** Others let no light pass through. Those objects are **opaque.**

This picture has three coverings. Which one is opaque? Which is transparent? Which is translucent?

Pretend you're at a friend's party. Everyone takes home a piece of cake. Your friend wraps the cake in waxed paper. How clearly can you see the cake? The cake looks blurred because waxed paper is translucent.

Think of a wrap that is opaque. You might suggest aluminum foil or brown paper. What kind of wrap is transparent?

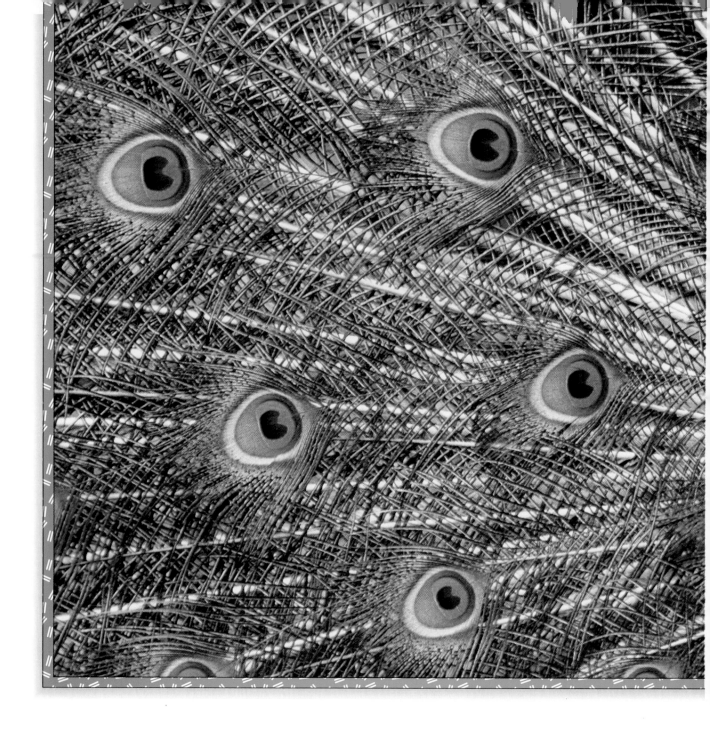

Look at the picture now. The coverings have been removed. You can clearly see what was under the opaque and translucent coverings.

The transparent covering is clear. When it covered the picture, you could still see what was under it. What other things are transparent? You might think of a window or clear water.

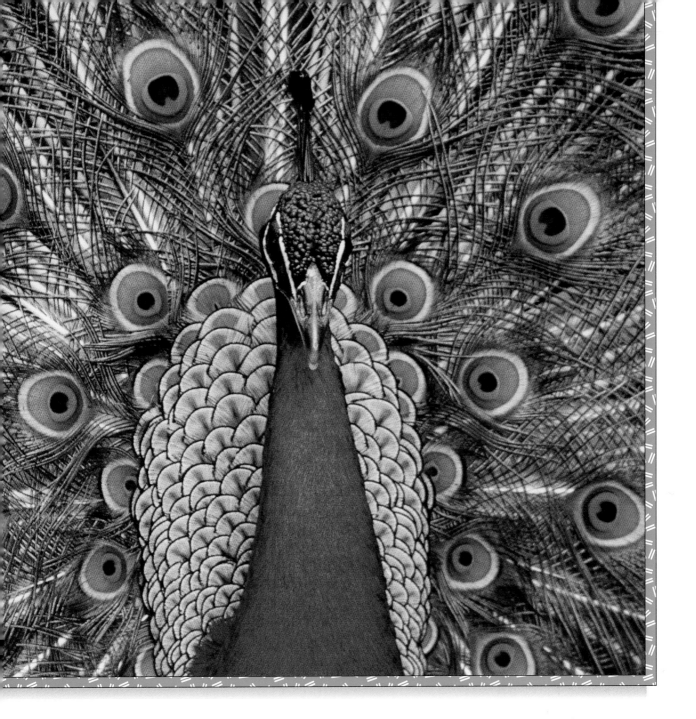

Suppose you are sitting at your desk and sunlight is shining in your eyes. You hold up a piece of writing paper to block the sun. Some sunlight comes through the paper. The paper is translucent.

You then hold up a book. No sunlight comes through the book. That's because the book blocks the sunlight. The book is opaque.

Looking at Shadows

WHAT YOU NEED

bag of objects

posterboard screen

overhead projector

Science Notebook

1. Choose an object from the bag. Don't let anyone see it. Place it behind the screen on the overhead projector.

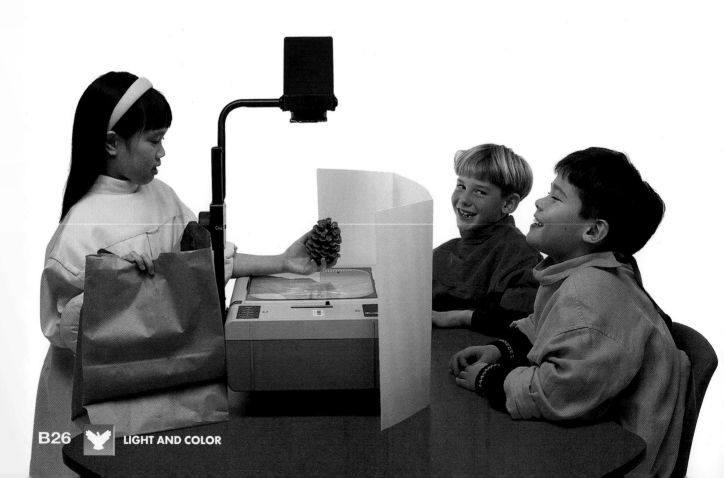

2. Darken the room. Turn on the projector. Have classmates guess what the object is by looking at its shadow.

3. After classmates have written their guesses, show the object. Talk about their guesses.

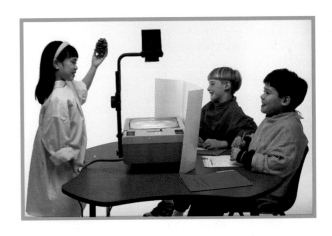

4. Take turns repeating steps 1, 2, and 3.

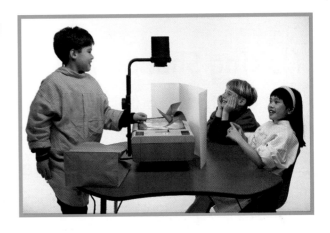

Think! How were you able to guess an object without really seeing it?

Making Shadows

The picture shows shadow animals. They are made by shining a light on an opaque object. The object blocks the light and makes a **shadow.**

You can make shadows, too. Stand in front of a light. Face away from the light. Look at your shadow on the wall.

SHADOW ZOO

Can you make your shadow move? Wiggle your arms. Shake your head. How does your shadow change?

Now look at your hand. It blocks the light. That's because your hand is opaque. It makes a shadow on the wall. Turn the page to find out how to use your hands to make shadow animals.

The shadow of two hands spread out makes a
butterfly or bird. The shadow of one hand on top of
another looks like an elephant. Can you see its trunk?

The alligator is the shadow of the palms of two
hands held together. The shadow of an arm and hand
makes a swan. What shadows can you make?

SHADOW ZOO

Try making a bunny shadow. Make a fist with one hand. Point two fingers to make the ears. How can you make your bunny shadow hop?

A shadow is made when a light shines on an opaque object. Look for shadows outdoors and indoors. You'll find them all around you when the light is right.

Making Shadows Change

WHAT YOU NEED

newsprint

lump of clay

pencil

plastic-foam ball

flashlight

marker

Science Notebook

1. Spread newsprint on your desk. Place clay in the center of the newsprint.

2. Push a pencil into a plastic-foam ball. Stand the pencil and ball in the lump of clay.

LIGHT AND COLOR

3. Darken the room. Shine a flashlight on the ball. Mark where the shadow falls on the newsprint.

4. Move the light around. Mark where the shadow falls on the newsprint each time. Record your observations.

Think! How does the shadow change when you move the light?

Shadows Can Change

Shadow length depends on where the light is. The light could be to one side of an opaque object. It could be near or far, high or low.

The first picture was taken in the morning. The sun is low in the sky. A low light makes a long shadow.

LIGHT AND COLOR

Look at the second picture. Imagine it's noontime, when the sun is high in the sky. Will the shadows be longer than in the morning, or shorter? When light comes from high up, objects make short shadows.

Later in the day the sun will be low in the sky. Then shadows will be long again.

Catching Colors

WHAT YOU NEED

white posterboard   clear plastic jar of water   mirror

flashlight   crayons   Science Notebook

1. Hold white paper a few inches from a plastic jar of water. Place a mirror at an angle in the plastic jar.

2. Darken the room. Shine a flashlight on the mirror. Move the light around until you see colors on the white paper.

3. Draw what you see, using crayons the same colors as the colors on the white paper.

Think! Where do the colors come from?

Making Rainbows

It has just finished raining. The sun is shining through the clouds. Look at the sky. You see lines of different colors. These lines of colors are called a **rainbow.** The colors of a rainbow are red, orange, yellow, green, blue, indigo, and violet.

When it rains, drops of water in the air act like prisms. A **prism** is clear glass or plastic that is shaped like a pyramid.

White light passing through a prism bends. Sunlight passing through drops of water also bends. This light splits into the colors of the rainbow.

Mixing Colors

WHAT YOU NEED

large white paper (optional)

2 cups of blue water

2 cups of
red water

1 cup of
yellow water

1 cup of
green water

crayons

Science Notebook

1. Predict what color the water will become when you mix blue water and red water. Record your prediction.

2. Mix blue water and red water together. Record what you see.

3. Repeat steps 1 and 2, using blue water and yellow water.

4. Repeat steps 1 and 2, using green water and red water.

Think! What did you learn about mixing colors to make new colors?

Making New Colors

Color is missing from parts of this picture. Colors can help us tell what things are.

The many colors on this page were made by mixing red, yellow, and blue. By mixing these colors you can make all the other colors.

The toucans are going to add the missing colors to this page. One toucan has red paint and blue paint. Another has red paint and yellow paint. What colors do the other toucans have?

When the toucans mix their paints, what colors will they get? If you turn the page, you'll find out.

The toucan that mixed red and blue paints made purple paint. He painted the flower. Find the toucan that mixed yellow and red. He painted the tiger orange. What colors were mixed to paint the snake? Blue and yellow were mixed to make green.

The monkey was painted brown. What colors were mixed to make brown?

How can you know which colors of paint to mix?
The order of colors in the rainbow can help you.
Orange is between red and yellow. You make orange
paint by mixing red and yellow. Green is between
yellow and blue in the rainbow. What colors should
you mix to make green? What colors would you mix to
make purple?

Word Power

A. Match the words with a picture.

transparent   translucent   opaque

a.    b.    c.

B. Use these words to fill in the blanks.

beam   light   reflects   prism
straight   shadow   heat   rainbow

1. A transparent object lets _____ pass through.
2. When drops of water in the sky break sunlight into different colors, a _____ forms.
3. When an object blocks light, you get a _____.
4. Light travels in a _____ line.
5. Stars give off both light and _____.
6. The moon _____ the light of the sun.
7. A flashlight sends out a _____ of light.
8. A _____ splits white light into colors.

Using Science Ideas

Explain where the light source is in each picture. What clues help you know the location of the light source?

a.

b.

Solving Science Problems

1. If the lights go out at night, what natural sources of light could you use?

2. Explain how white light splits into colors and what the order of the colors is.

3. Make a chart like the one shown. Fill in the colors you would get.

Colors you mix	Color you get
red and yellow	
red and blue	
yellow and blue	

UNIT C

EARTH THROUGH TIME

Themes: Models; Scale; Constancy and Change

Examining
Dinosaur Models

WHAT YOU NEED

dinosaur models

hand lens

Science Notebook

1. Choose two very different
dinosaur models.

2. Look carefully at each model.

3. Draw the two dinosaurs you chose.

4. Write words to describe each one.

Think! How are the dinosaur models alike, and how are they different?

Diplodocus

Ornitholestes

All About Dinosaurs

Millions of years ago, **dinosaurs** lived on the earth. There were many kinds. Allosaurus had a big 36-inch (91-centimeter) head. Ornitholestes had a small 6-inch (15-centimeter) head. All dinosaurs had four limbs. Brachiosaurus walked on all four legs. Its front legs were longer than its back legs.

Brachiosaurus

Allosaurus

Allosaurus walked on two legs. Its front limbs were shorter. They had sharp claws. The front limbs were used to grab and hold food.

Different dinosaurs ate different kinds of foods. Diplodocus ate plants. Allosaurus ate other dinosaurs. Ornitholestes also ate meat. Dinosaurs were like each other. Yet they were different in many ways.

Comparing
Sizes of Dinosaurs

WHAT YOU NEED

dinosaur pictures

yardstick

Science Notebook

1. Stand next to the dinosaur picture on the wall and compare the size of the dinosaur to your size.

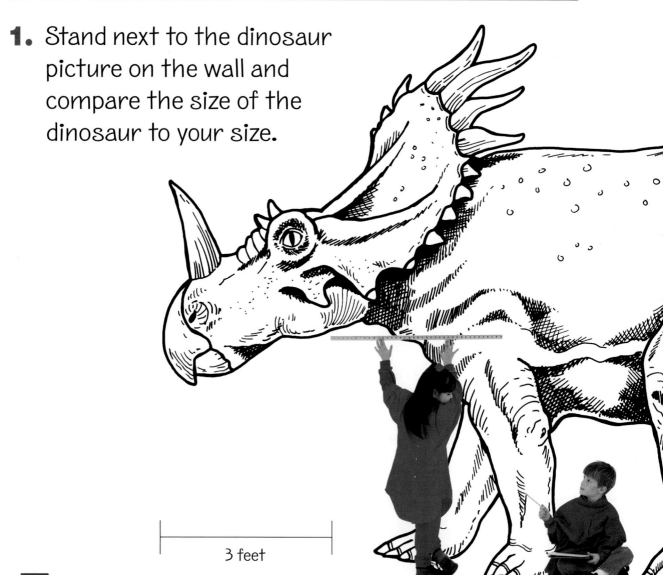

3 feet

2. Measure the length of the dinosaur. Record the length.

3. Repeat steps 1 and 2 for each dinosaur picture.

4. Make a bar graph to compare the lengths of the dinosaurs.

Think! Which dinosaurs were bigger than you?

Lambeosaurus

Dinosaur Sizes

Dinosaurs were many sizes. This picture compares them to things we know today. Find Lambeosaurus. It's about 50 feet (15 meters) long. That's longer than a boxcar! Now find Triceratops. It's 30 feet (9 meters) long. That's as long as a school bus! Look at the size of Velociraptor. It's only 8 feet (2.4 meters) long.

Triceratops

Velociraptor

There were dinosaurs bigger and smaller than these. The smallest, Compsognathus, was the size of a chicken. It was about 30 inches (76 centimeters) long.

Seismosaurus was the longest at 170 feet (51 meters). That's twice as long as a basketball court! One of the largest, Brachiosaurus, weighed 40 tons (36 metric tons). That's as much as 10 hippopotamuses.

Examining Fossils

2 fossils

hand lens

Science Notebook

1. Look closely at two fossils. Record what you see.

2. Discuss what kinds of living things made these fossils. Decide if they were plants or animals when they were alive.

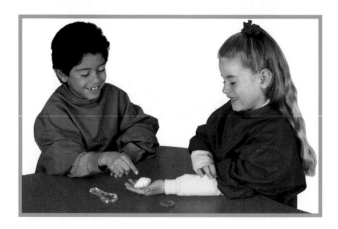

3. Draw how you think these plants or animals looked.

Think! How are the two fossils alike, and how are they different?

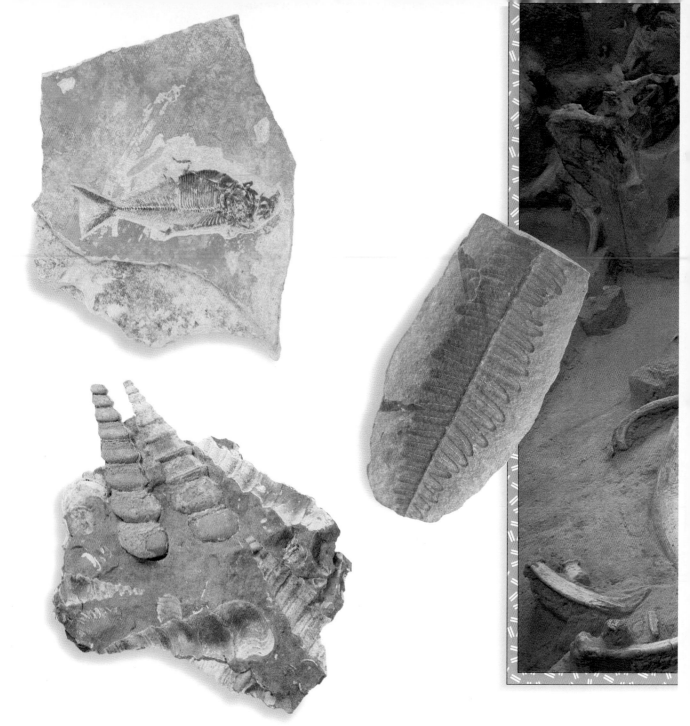

All About Fossils

Fossils are the remains or imprints of once-living things. **Remains** are parts of the living thing.

Find the remains in the picture. The bones are remains. They are from a mammoth. Scientists use these remains. They build models of animals with them. Models show what each animal looked like.

Find the imprints in the picture. There's a fish imprint. It shows the exact size and shape of the fish.

Fossil imprints work like rubber stamps. When you press an inked stamp on paper, you get an imprint. A leaf pressed in mud leaves an imprint, too. Imprints of dinosaur skin have been found. They show what dinosaur skin looked like.

Comparing Imprints

WHAT YOU NEED

goggles

dough

paper plate

hand lens

once-living objects

fossil imprint

Science Notebook

1. Flatten a piece of dough on a paper plate.

2. Press each object into the dough and carefully remove it.

3. Look closely at each imprint. Record what you see.

4. Compare your imprints with a fossil imprint.

Think! How are your imprints different from the fossil imprint?

Fossil Imprints

Fossil imprints form in mud or other matter that later hardens. Imagine the earth many years ago. A dinosaur walked on soft ground. Footprints were left. They turned to stone. Years later they're found. The footprints give clues about the size of the dinosaur and the shape of its feet.

Remains of plants can also become fossil imprints. Millions of years ago, leaves began to rot in a swamp. The leaves were covered by dirt. The pressure of the dirt changed the leaves to peat. More pressure turned the peat to coal. Leaf imprints were found in the coal. They show what the plants from many years ago looked like.

Comparing
Handprints

WHAT YOU NEED

goggles

dough

ruler

paper plate

mystery handprint

Science Notebook

1. Flatten dough on a paper plate.

2. Spread your fingers apart. Carefully make a handprint in the dough.

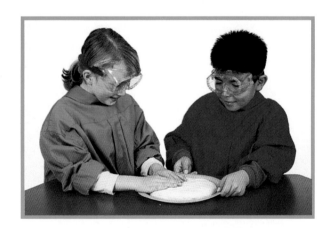

3. Measure your handprint. Record the measurements.

4. Measure the mystery handprint. Record the measurements.

5. Compare your handprint to the mystery handprint.

Think! What clues does each handprint give you?

Fossil Footprints

Scientists study fossil footprints. The footprints are clues to how big dinosaurs were.

Look at the footprints above. What can help you match each footprint to the dinosaur that made it? You might look at the size of the footprint. You might look at the shape of the foot. You might count the toes.

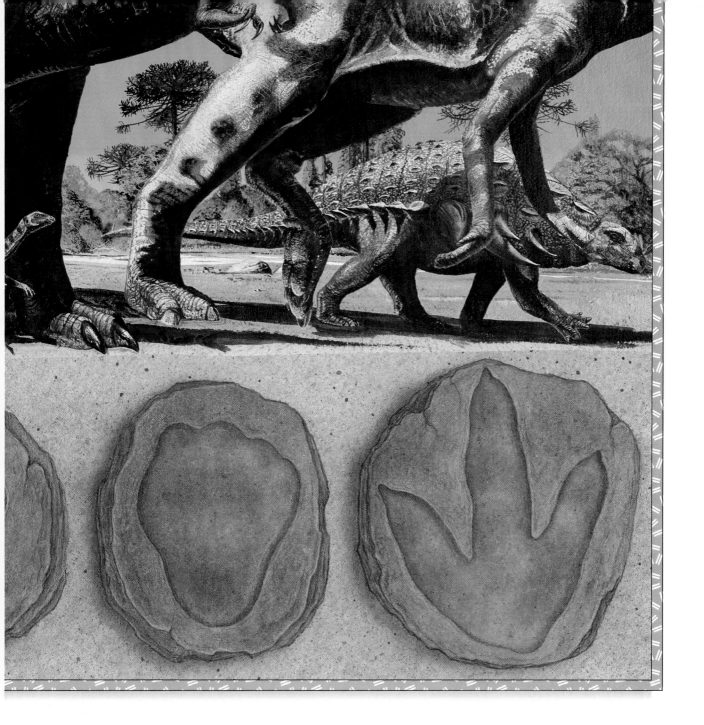

Imagine you are walking in the woods. You find small footprints. What can you tell about the animal that made those footprints? You might guess it was a very small animal.

Scientists compare footprints. In the same soil, the heavier animal left the deeper imprint. In harder soils, that same animal might leave shallow prints.

Finding
Remains in Sand

WHAT YOU NEED

goggles

newspapers

tray of sand

plastic spoons

paper plates

Science Notebook

1. Pretend you're a scientist digging for animal remains.

2. Dig carefully in the sand, one spoonful at a time.

3. Place sand on one of the paper plates.

4. Place any remains you find on another paper plate.

5. Record your findings.

Think! What can you learn from the remains you found?

Stenonychosaurus

Ankylosaurus

Things Fossils Tell Us

Dinosaurs like these died long ago. Mud covered them. The soft parts of their bodies rotted. Only their bones remained. Years passed. The bones turned to stone. Later, scientists dug up the **fossil remains.** Scientists recreated the dinosaurs with these bones.

Ouranosaurus

Bones tell how long a dinosaur's legs were. They show the shape of its head. They even let us know what its neck looked like.

Look at the large bones. They belong to the large dinosaur. The small bones belong to the small dinosaur. By fitting bones together, scientists can tell how a dinosaur stood and walked.

Comparing
Kinds of Teeth

WHAT YOU NEED

goggles

2 tree leaves

2 golf tees

2 small blocks of wood

timer

dry cereal

Science Notebook

1. Pretend the blocks are flat teeth. Grind a leaf between two blocks for 1 minute. Record how the leaf changed.

2. Pretend the golf tees are pointed teeth. Tear the second leaf for 1 minute. Record how the leaf changed.

3. Repeat steps 1 and 2, using the cereal.

Think! What do flat teeth do better and what do pointed teeth do better?

Dinosaur Teeth

Look at the mouths of the dinosaurs. Point to their teeth. Look at the dinosaur in the back. Why can't you see its teeth? They are too far back in its mouth.

Which dinosaur will eat the plant? It needs blunt, **flat teeth** to grind the food. Which will eat the lizard? It needs sharp, **pointed teeth** to tear the food.

Scientists can tell what foods some dinosaurs ate. They look at the shape and sharpness of the teeth.

Most plant-eating dinosaurs had blunt, flat teeth to crush the plants. Most meat eaters had sharp, pointed teeth to tear the meat. Some dinosaurs had 2,000 teeth in their mouth. Turn the page to see the teeth of the dinosaurs in the picture.

Edmontosaurus

This picture shows the skulls of the dinosaurs. The **skulls** show the teeth. Edmontosaurus had blunt, flat teeth. Its teeth were good for grinding food. It was a plant eater.

Albertosaurus's long jaw had many pointed teeth. The teeth were sharp like a knife for cutting meat. Albertosaurus was a meat eater.

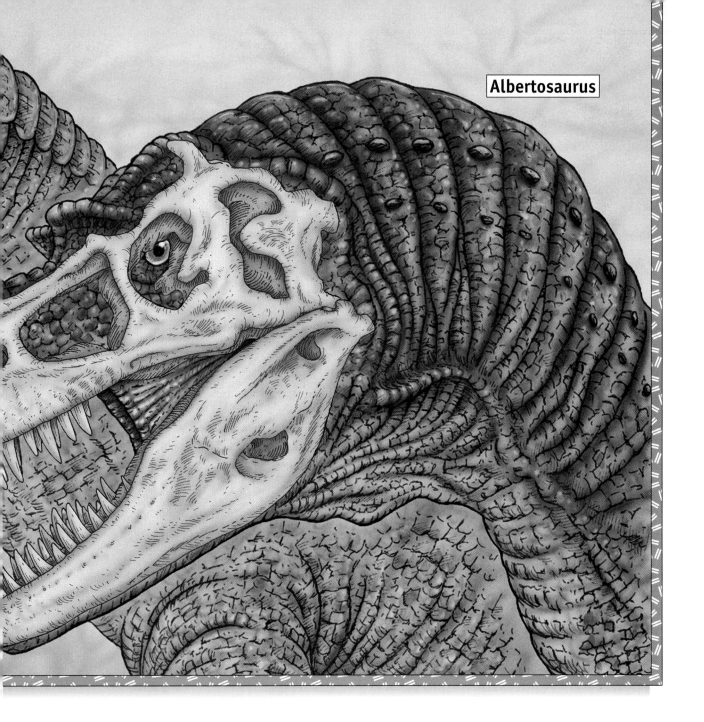

Most people know about Tyrannosaurus. It had teeth that were 6 inches (15 centimeters) long. They were pointed like knives. The teeth had edges like a saw. What do you think Tyrannosaurus ate?

Some toothless dinosaurs had bills. They used their bills to catch worms, insects, and soft lizards. Other toothless dinosaurs ate plants.

Assembling a Dinosaur Skeleton

WHAT YOU NEED

dinosaur skeleton pieces

tape

Science Notebook

1. Spread the dinosaur skeleton pieces on the table.

2. Tape the parts together to make a skeleton.

3. Draw a picture of what you think this dinosaur looked like.

Think! What can you tell about the dinosaur from its skeleton?

Looking at Skeletons

Think about putting together a puzzle. Dinosaur bones are like pieces of a puzzle. Scientists find a few dinosaur bones at a time. They put the bones together to make a **skeleton.** Scientists use real bones to build skeletons. The model then is the exact size and shape of the dinosaur.

Imagine what scientists learn as they build skeletons. They don't only learn about a dinosaur's size and shape. They learn about other things as well.

Look at the skeleton of Corythosaurus. Its back legs are much larger than its front legs. What might this mean? It probably walked on two legs. Turn the page to see how this dinosaur might have looked.

An artist drew this picture. It shows how Corythosaurus might have looked. What else can you tell about this dinosaur?

Look at the head. It has a crest. The crest might have been used to scare away other animals. It might have been used to make sounds. What other clues might skeletons give?

Scientists found a reptile with wings. It was covered with feathers. It might not have been able to fly. But it could climb. Scientists think that reptiles may be early relatives of birds.

Skeletons of whole families of dinosaurs have been found together. Scientists think this shows that some dinosaurs cared for their young.

Comparing
Dinosaurs and Living Animals

WHAT YOU NEED

dinosaur cards   living-animal cards   Science Notebook

1. Match each dinosaur card with a living-animal card.

2. Draw the matching pairs.

3. Record how the dinosaur and living
animal in each pair are alike.

**Think! How can living animals help
us learn about dinosaurs?**

Extinct and Endangered

Dinosaurs became **extinct** long ago. They can no longer be found on the earth. Yet some animals alive today are like dinosaurs. Some dinosaurs used beaks and claws to tear their food. Owls do that. Many dinosaur footprints were found in one place. This may mean that dinosaurs lived in herds. Cattle live in herds.

Scarlet Macaws

Some animals today are as fun to learn about as dinosaurs. Yet many are in danger of no longer existing. The birds shown are **endangered**. How can you help animals like these? You can help save the places where they live. You can also help save the places where they get food. Let's keep these and other animals from becoming extinct.

Word Power

A. Match the words with a picture.

fossil imprint   fossil remains

a.

b.

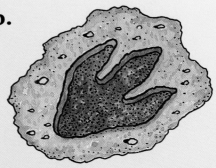

B. Use these words to fill in the blanks.

dinosaurs   skeleton   endangered   fossils
flat teeth   pointed teeth   extinct   skull

1. You study a dinosaur's _____ to see its teeth.

2. Animals that have _____ can tear food.

3. The bones of an animal make up its _____.

4. Millions of years ago, _____ lived on the earth.

5. Animals that have _____ can grind food.

6. Animals that are in danger of no longer existing
are _____.

7. The remains or imprints of once-living things are
called _____.

8. Animals that can no longer be found on the earth
are _____.

Using Science Ideas

What two things can you tell about this dinosaur by looking at its skeleton?

Solving Science Problems

1. How can you tell if a fossil is remains or an imprint?

2. What are two ways that scientists get clues about dinosaurs?

3. What can you do to help endangered animals from becoming extinct?

UNIT D

SOLIDS, LIQUIDS, AND GASES

Theme: Constancy and Change

Describing and Grouping
Solids

WHAT YOU NEED

marble

piece of wood

piece of metal

lid

piece of plastic

ball

button

paper clip

counter

Science Notebook

1. Look at and touch the solid objects.

2. Group the objects that are alike in some way.

3. Draw and name each group.

4. Group the objects in a different way. Draw and name each group.

Think! **What makes an object a solid?**

All About Solids

How are the objects in the picture alike? They are made of **matter**. They are solids. A **solid** does not change shape or size when it is moved.

You can describe a solid by its color, shape, size, and texture. The plate is blue and round. It is larger than the cup but smaller than the hat.

The **texture** of an object describes how it feels when you touch it. The plate feels smooth.

You can use color, shape, size, or texture to group solids. The plate, the cup, and the coffeepot are all blue objects. The log and the rope have rough textures. Which would you group together by shape? Which would you group by size?

Describing and Grouping Liquids

=== WHAT YOU NEED ===

goggles

cup of corn oil

cup of vegetable oil

cup of orange juice

cup of water

cup of colored water

cup of cola

cup of seltzer water

paper towels

Science Notebook

1. Look at each liquid and talk about the color.

2. Gently touch each liquid with your fingers and talk about the texture.

3. Group the liquids that are alike in some way.

4. Draw and name each group.

Think! What makes something a liquid?

All About Liquids

Do you like to drink liquids? A **liquid** is matter that
changes shape when it is moved to another container.
Each liquid takes the shape of the glass it is in. If you
pour a liquid from a tall glass into one that is short and
wide, the liquid will take the shape of the short glass.
The liquid still takes up the same amount of space.

How can you describe a liquid? One way is by its color. Milk and grape juice are liquids of different colors. Milk is white. Grape juice is purple. What colors are some other liquids?

A liquid can also be described by its texture. Cooking oil feels slippery. Other liquids feel smooth or sticky. What liquids have felt sticky to you?

Looking at Shapes

cup of water

cup with marble

jar A

jar B

paper towels

Science Notebook

1. Pour the water into jar A and record its shape.

2. Pour the water from jar A into jar B and record its shape.

3. Then pour the water back into the cup.

4. Put the marble into each jar and record the marble's shape each time.

Think! How are the shapes of the water and the marble different?

Looking at Shapes

You know that a solid has a definite shape. You also know that a liquid does not. A liquid takes the shape of the container it is in. You can use what you know to tell if something is a solid or a liquid.

Look at the picture. What is in each container? Does each container have a solid or a liquid in it?

SOLIDS, LIQUIDS, AND GASES

Is the flashlight a solid or a liquid? It is a solid because it has a definite shape. It does not take the shape of its container. If you put the flashlight into another container, it won't change shape.

Does the pitcher with blue matter in it hold a solid or a liquid? It holds a liquid. You can tell because the matter takes the shape of the container it is in.

Trapping Air

plastic bags

twist ties

Science Notebook

1. Swish one bag through the air to fill it. Close it quickly and tie it with a twist tie.

2. Look at the air inside the bag. Record how it looks.

D14 SOLIDS, LIQUIDS, AND GASES

3. Open the bag and smell the air. Record its smell.

4. Record the shape and color of the air as you let it out of the bag.

5. Repeat steps 1–4 with the other bags.

Think! What makes air a gas?

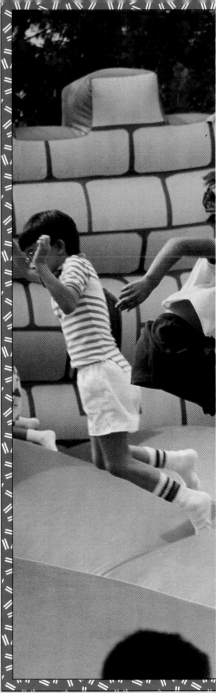

All About Gases

Gas is matter that is all around you and fills many kinds of things. Look at the pictures. There are gases in the balloons, the bubbles, and the ball. Gases fill the walls and floor of the funhouse.

Air is a gas that is all around the children. Air is all around you right now. You cannot see air.

SOLIDS, LIQUIDS, AND GASES

A gas does not have a set shape. A gas fills a container and takes its shape. A gas can also change the shape of some containers. As gas is added to a balloon, the balloon changes shape.

Not all containers change shape when a gas is added. Think about blowing air into a glass jar. The jar does not change shape.

Looking at Space

WHAT YOU NEED

plastic bottle

container with water

cup of water

marble

Science Notebook

1. Hold a bottle with the opening toward your partner's arm. Squeeze the bottle and record what happens.

2. Quickly push the bottle under the surface of the water in the container. Record what happens.

3. Put a marble into a cup of water. Record what happens.

Think! What happens when you try to put two kinds of matter into the same space?

Taking Up Space

Look at this beach picture. The chair, the ball, the toys, the drink holder, and the sand are all solids. The ocean and the juice inside the drink holder are liquids.

You cannot see the gases in the picture. The ball is filled with gas. The air, which is all around everything in the picture, is a gas.

All objects—solids, liquids, and gases—are made of matter. All matter takes up space. Think about which object in the picture takes up the largest space. The ocean might be your choice. Or maybe you think it's the air or the beach.

Now think about which matter takes up the smallest space. Maybe it's one tiny grain of sand.

Making
Ice Warmer

WHAT YOU NEED

cup with ice cubes

Science Notebook

1. Look at the ice cubes. Talk about their size, shape, color, and texture.

2. Decide whether ice cubes are a solid, a liquid, or a gas. Tell why you think so.

SOLIDS, LIQUIDS, AND GASES

3. Think of a plan to make ice cubes warmer. Record your plan.

4. Predict what will happen. Record your prediction and test it.

Think! What happens when you make ice cubes warmer?

Solids Change to Liquids

Are these objects solids, liquids, or gases? They are solids. Think of ways you can describe their color, shape, size, and texture. There are yellow bananas, lemons, and ice pops. The blueberries, oranges, and limes are round. The raspberries and blueberries are small. The ice pops and bananas are smooth.

What are the ice pops made of? You probably know they are made of ice. Ice is the solid form of water. Think of what you know about ice. What can happen to ice on a lake when the sun heats it?

Heat can make solid matter change form. What will happen to the solid ice pops if heat is added to them? Turn the page to find out.

How have the ice pops changed? They have melted. The air around the ice pops was warm. This **heat** made the solid ice pops change form.

Parts of some ice pops are not yet melted. What will happen if the ice pops stay in the warm air? All of the ice pops will probably melt.

SOLIDS, LIQUIDS, AND GASES

The melted ice pops have taken the shape of their plates. How is this a clue that the solid ice pops have become liquid?

You know that ice is the solid form of water. When ice is heated, it changes to liquid water. Where should you keep an ice pop if you do not want it to melt?

Observing
Water

WHAT YOU NEED

2 cups

container of water

plastic wrap

tape

grease pencil

Science Notebook

1. Put the same amount of water in each cup.

2. Mark the water levels.

3. Cover one cup. Put both cups in a sunny place.

4. Wait one day. Look at the cups. Record what you see.

Think! How has the water in each cup changed?

Liquids Change to Gases

Cooling off in water can be fun. The children in the picture are spraying each other with water from a hose. What are some other ways you use water?

What can these children do to get dry if they do not have a towel? They can dry in the sun. They might run around and let the air dry them.

Where does the water go when children dry in the sun? The liquid water on the children's skin changes from a liquid to a gas. The gas is called **water vapor.** You cannot see water vapor.

A liquid **evaporates** when it changes to a gas. How do you feel when water evaporates from your skin? You usually feel cooler and drier.

Making Rain

jar of very
warm water

newspapers

pie pan
with ice

Science Notebook

1. Feel the pie pan and the jar. Talk about
how each feels.

2. Carefully place the pie pan on top of
the jar of water.

3. Predict what you think will happen
inside the jar. Record your prediction.

4. Watch the jar. Record what happens.

Think! How did the water in the jar change?

Gases Change to Liquids

You know that there is air all around. Air is a gas that you can't see. Water vapor is another gas. You can't see it. There is water vapor in the air.

Where does the water vapor in air come from? Water vapor forms when water evaporates. Look at the picture. Where might water vapor come from?

Water from the river warms. It evaporates and changes to water vapor. The water vapor rises into the air. As it rises, the water vapor in air becomes cooler and cooler.

When water vapor becomes cool enough, it changes to liquid water. A gas **condenses** when it changes to a liquid.

Look what has been added to this picture. Find the arrow that points up from the river. It is wavy. This arrow shows water evaporating from the river. Follow the arrow to the sky. What do you see above the buildings?

As water vapor rises, it cools. The water vapor condenses into tiny water drops. The tiny drops of liquid water in the air form clouds.

SOLIDS, LIQUIDS, AND GASES

Sometimes the tiny water drops in clouds form larger drops. Large and heavy drops fall as rain. Where does rain fall?

Water evaporates from the river. It condenses and forms clouds. The water in clouds falls back to the earth. Some of the water evaporates again. These changes in water are called the **water cycle.**

Changing Water

cup   container of water   grease pencil   Science Notebook

1. Put water into the cup. Mark the water level.

2. Place the cup of water in a freezer overnight. Predict what will happen.

3. Observe the cup the next morning. Record what you see.

4. Observe the cup during the day. Look at the level of the water. Record what you see.

Think! What do you notice about the amount of water in the cup?

pouring

mixing

Liquids Change to Solids

Many things were once a different kind of matter than they are now. The pictures show the steps in making crayons. Look at the first picture. It shows liquid wax. Wax was heated to make it **melt.**

Now look at the second picture. It shows color being mixed into the liquid wax.

moving along

sorting

Look at the last two pictures. Here the crayons have changed from liquid to solid. The liquid wax is poured into molds shaped like crayons. As it cools, the liquid changes to a solid.

A liquid **freezes** when it changes to a solid. Juice can become an ice pop when it cools enough to freeze. What other liquids freeze into useful solids?

Exploring
Goo

goggles    cup of goo   plastic jar   Science Notebook

1. Look at, touch, and smell the goo. Try to pour it into the jar.

2. Decide if goo is a solid, a liquid, or a gas. Record what you think it is and why.

3. Make a plan for changing the goo. Record your plan.

4. Predict and record what you think will happen.

5. Carry out your plan and compare your findings to your prediction.

Think! How did the goo change and why?

Matter Everywhere

Matter is all around you. A solid has a definite size. It also has a definite shape. A liquid has a definite amount. It does not have a definite shape. Gases have no definite size or shape.

Look at the picture. Find solids, liquids, and gases. The next page gives you some examples. Can you find more?

SOLIDS, LIQUIDS, AND GASES

Solids The buildings, the plants, the signs, the stove, and the bathtub are some of the solids.

Liquids The milk in the baby's bottle, the water in the bathtub and sink, the bubble liquid, and the drops that make up the clouds are liquids.

Gases The balloons, the blimp, the bubbles, and the ball have gas in them.

Word Power

A. Match the words with a picture.

solid   liquid   gas

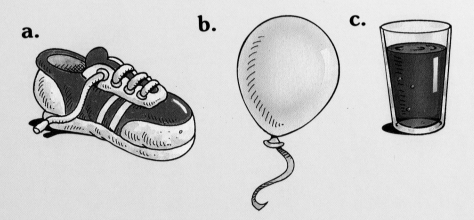

a.   **b.**   **c.**

B. Use these words to fill in the blanks.

matter   water vapor   heat   evaporates
freezes   condenses   texture   melts

1. All objects are made of _____.

2. When a liquid changes to a solid, it _____.

3. When a liquid changes to a gas, it _____.

4. When a gas changes to a liquid, it _____.

5. How something feels is its _____.

6. When a solid changes to a liquid, it _____.

7. When water is a gas, it is called _____.

8. Energy that can change a solid to a liquid
is called _____.

Using Science Ideas

How many solids, liquids, and gases can you find in the picture? List them.

Solving Science Problems

1. Why do crayons melt in a hot car?

2. Describe one way that matter changes form.

3. Make a chart like the one shown. Add more objects to your chart. Put checks in the right places.

Object	Has its own shape	Takes the shape of its container	Spreads out to fill its container	Kind of matter
doll	✔			solid

UNIT E

WHAT MAKES ME SICK

Themes: Systems; Scale

Making Clay Models

WHAT YOU NEED

pictures of germs   clay   paper plate   Science Notebook

---

1. Study the microscope pictures of germs. Look at the shapes of the germs.

2. Use small pieces of clay to make models of the different germs you see.

3. Draw your models.

Think! How are your models like real germs? How are they different?

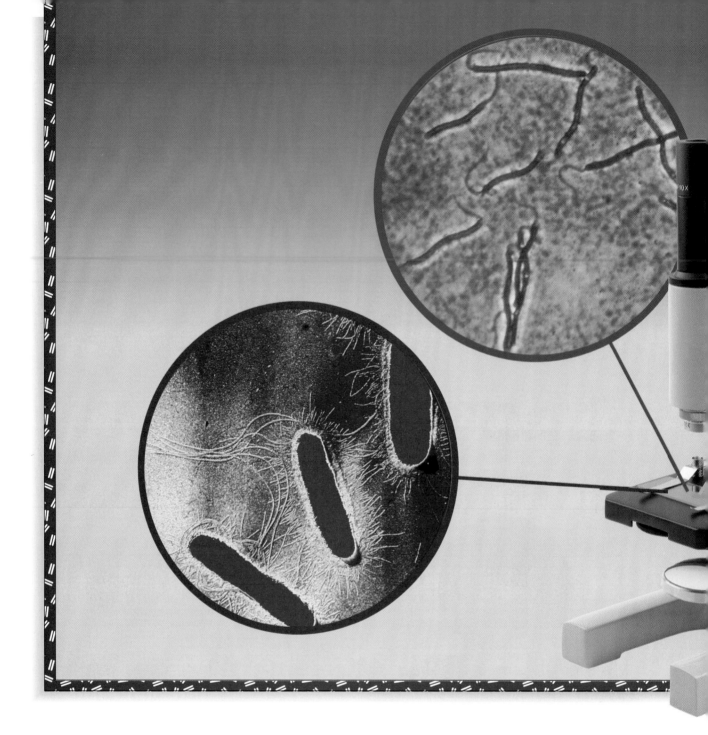

Looking at Germs

Germs can get inside your body. They can make
you sick. Bacteria and viruses are two kinds of germs.
You need to use a **microscope** to see bacteria.
Viruses are too small to be seen with most kinds of
microscopes. Look at the picture. It shows what
bacteria look like under a microscope.

Different germs cause different sicknesses. Two kinds of **viruses** cause colds and chickenpox. **Bacteria** cause some kinds of sore throats. Have you ever had a sickness caused by germs?

Do you know why you should learn about germs? Knowing about germs is one way you can help yourself and others stay healthy.

Examining a
Pretend Sneeze

WHAT YOU NEED

tape

sheet of plastic

spray bottle of water

paper towel

tissues

Science Notebook

1. Tape a sheet of plastic to a wall.

2. Use a spray bottle to spray water on the plastic. Record what you see on the plastic.

3. Use a paper towel to dry the plastic.

4. Hold a tissue between the spray bottle and the plastic. Try to spray water on the plastic.

5. Record what you see on the plastic. Compare your results.

Think! What did you see that surprised you?

Sneezing Spreads Germs

The picture shows a boy sneezing. It begins with the boy throwing back his head. It ends with the boy sneezing into his hands. As he **sneezes**, air and liquid come out of his nose and mouth. There are germs in the liquid. The large circle shows how these germs look under a microscope.

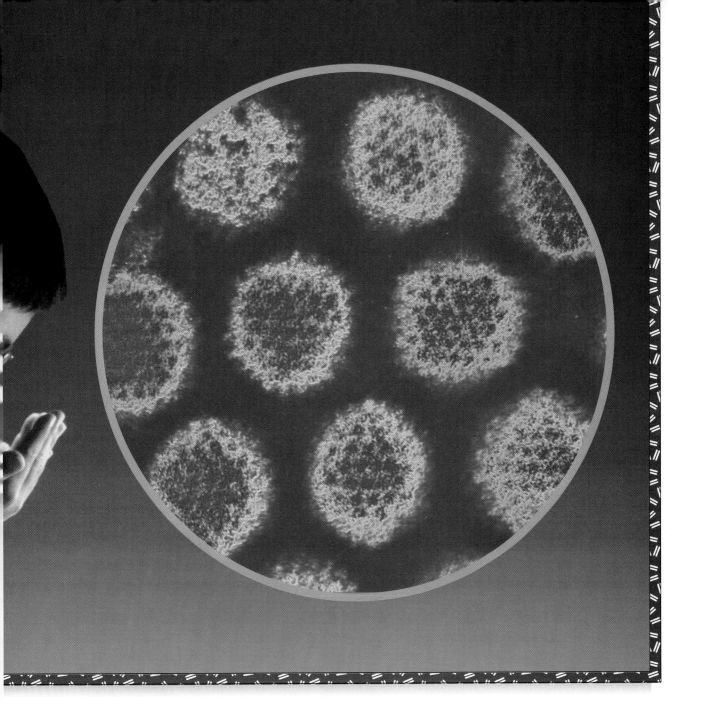

What are some ways to keep germs from spreading when you sneeze? You can cover your nose and mouth with your hands as the boy in the picture is doing.

You can also hold a tissue over your nose and mouth. Then you should put the tissue in the trash. You should use soap and water to wash the germs off your hands.

Understanding
How Germs Are Spread

WHAT YOU NEED

goggles

piece of stick candy

paper plate

red chalk dust

cup of water

cotton swabs

Science Notebook

1. Dip a piece of candy in water and roll it in the red chalk dust on the paper plate.

2. Roll the candy in your hands.

3. Predict what will happen when you shake hands with a classmate. Shake hands.

4. Rub a moist cotton swab on your hand. Record what you see on the cotton swab.

Think! If the red chalk dust were germs, in what other ways could germs be spread?

Germs Everywhere

Look at the picture. Think about places where you might find germs. There are germs everywhere. All the objects—the books, notebooks, pencils, scissors, paper clips, erasers, and table—have germs on them. Germs are very small. Even though you cannot see germs, you know they are there.

How do you think germs spread to the objects in the picture? Some germs come from the hands of people who touch the objects.

People may sneeze near the objects. If they do not cover their noses and mouths, germs get on the objects. Then when someone picks up one of the objects, germs **spread** to his or her hands.

This picture shows some of the germs that could be on the objects. These germs are shown just as you would see them under a microscope.

Arrows point to places where the germs might be. It looks like there are a lot of germs in the circles. There are really many more. Remember, germs are very small.

What are some ways you can keep germs from spreading? You can wash the desk. You can wash your hands. You can decide not to share books, pencils, and erasers. You can cover your nose and mouth with a tissue when you sneeze. You can also keep things that don't normally go in your mouth out of your mouth.

Examining
How Dust Collects

WHAT YOU NEED

waxed paper

petroleum jelly

index card with string

hand lens

Science Notebook

---

1. Use waxed paper to spread petroleum jelly on an index card.

2. Examine the index card with a hand lens. Record what you see.

3. Hang the card where moving air will blow on it.

4. Repeat step 2 after two days. Compare your results.

Think! What changed the surface of the card?

Trapping Germs

Look at the picture of the girl playing baseball. She is kicking up dust as she slides. What are the other children doing? They are also putting dust into the air.

Think about how it feels to breathe with dust in the air. Dust can make it hard to breathe. Dust has germs in it. So dust puts germs into the air.

What are some ways your body protects you from germs? One way is by trapping dust and germs in mucus. **Mucus** is a sticky material in your nose, mouth, and throat.

Mucus helps trap dust and germs to keep them from getting further into your body. Germs cannot make you sick if they cannot get into your body.

Preventing
Germs From Spreading

Science Notebook

1. Talk to your school nurse about germs and how they are spread.

2. Find places where germs might be spread.

3. Record what you observe.

4. Think about what can be done to stop the spread of germs in school.

5. Write a plan. Carry out your plan.

Think! How could you prevent germs from spreading in your home?

Protect Yourself

Think about how germs might be spread in each picture. The first boy has cut his knee. Germs can get inside his body through the cut. The girls are drinking from the same straw. They are sharing germs. The last boy is about to pick up an apple core. It has on it the germs of the person that ate it.

WHAT MAKES ME SICK

What can be done to keep germs from spreading?
The first boy can wash the cut with soap and water.
Then he can put a bandage on it to keep it clean. Each
girl should have her own drink.

The last boy should use a napkin or paper towel to
pick up the apple core and throw it away. Then he
should wash his hands with soap and water.

Examining
Health and Safety

WHAT YOU NEED

crayons

Science Notebook

1. Draw a cartoon strip.

2. First, show someone who is sick or injured.

3. Next, show what could be done to make that person healthy again.

4. Last, show how the sickness or injury could have been prevented.

Think! What community helpers do you need when you are sick or injured?

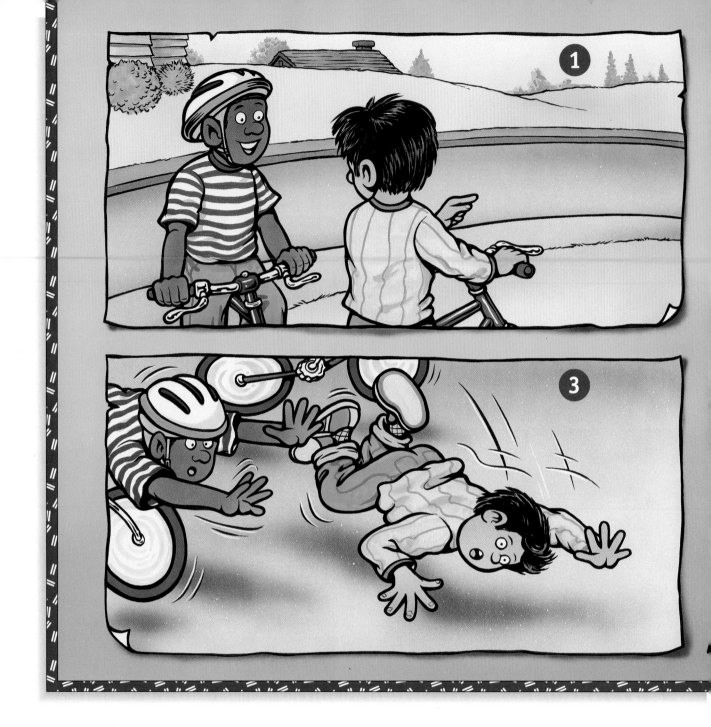

Preventing Injury

Look at the picture story. What happened? One of the boys hit his head on the sidewalk. He has an **injury**. Why does one boy have an injury but the other boy does not? The boy that hurt his head was not wearing a safety helmet. The boy without the injury was wearing a safety helmet.

WHAT MAKES ME SICK

The boy who hurt his head can **prevent**, or stop, an injury from happening again. He can wear a safety helmet. What else can the boy do to prevent an injury?

The boy can pedal slower. He can be careful to watch where he is going. The boy might even decide to wear elbow pads on his arms and knee pads on his legs.

Exploring
Healthful Activities

WHAT YOU NEED

magazine ads for
alcohol and cigarettes

markers

crayons

Science Notebook

1. Look at the ads for
   drinking and smoking.

2. Think of a healthful
   activity that could be
   done instead.

3. Draw an ad for your healthful activity.

4. Write how your activity will help people stay healthy.

Think! What are some other ways you can keep your body healthy?

Staying Healthy

What are some ways you can keep your body healthy? You can eat healthful foods. These kinds of foods help your body grow strong. You can also exercise. This will make your muscles and bones stronger.

Getting enough sleep helps keep you healthy, too. When you sleep, your body gets the rest it needs.

WHAT MAKES ME SICK

What are some things that are not good for your body? Too many cookies, candies, or potato chips are not good for you. Alcohol, cigarettes, and drugs are not good for you, either.

Follow the maze with your finger. Decide which things are good for your body. You will get to the finish by choosing healthful things.

Word Power

A. Match the words with a picture.
microscope   germs

b.

a.

B. Use these words to fill in the blanks.
bacteria   viruses   germs   prevent
injury   sneeze   spread   mucus

1. You wear a bicycle helmet to _____ an injury.

2. Germs that can be seen with a microscope are _____.

3. Germs that are too small to be seen with most kinds of microscopes are _____.

4. A scraped knee is an _____.

5. When you _____, you send germs into the air.

6. When you pick up an object, germs _____ to your hands.

7. If _____ get into your body they can make you sick.

8. A sticky material that helps keep germs from getting in your body is called _____.

Using Science Ideas

How are germs being spread? Make a list.

Solving Science Problems

1. Describe two ways that you can help germs from spreading to others when you are sick.

2. How does the body protect itself from germs?

3. Make a chart like the one shown. List activities and things that you can do to stay healthy. Add your own ideas to the chart.

Activities	Staying Healthy
Bike riding	Wear a bicycle helmet
Roller skating	
Sneezing	

SCIENCE Handbook

Think Like a Scientist

A scientist studies nature. A scientist thinks about ideas in a careful way. You can think like a scientist.

Observe

To think like a scientist, observe the things around you. Everything you hear and see is a clue about how the world works.

Roland and Shannon are playing with clay. They make the clay into many shapes. Roland places a clay ball into water. The clay ball sinks.

Ask a Question

As you observe, you may see that some things happen over and over. Ask questions about such things.

Roland says that the clay ball is too heavy to float. Shannon points out that heavy boats float. Roland wonders, how can we change the clay so it will float?

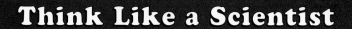

Make a Guess

Suppose you have an idea about why something happens. You make a guess based on your idea.

Shannon has an idea about what made the clay ball sink. She thinks that changing the shape of the clay might make the clay float.

Plan and Do a Test

After you make a guess, plan how to test it.
Then carry out your plan.

Roland and Shannon test the idea.
Roland makes the clay ball into a boat.
The boat has space inside it.
He puts the clay boat in water.

Write What Happens

You need to observe your test carefully. Then write down what happens.

Roland and Shannon watch the clay boat. They see that it floats. Shannon writes down what they did and what happened.

Draw Conclusions

Think about different reasons why something happened as it did.

Roland decides that the shape of the boat and the space inside help it float. The clay ball did not have a space inside and so the ball could not float.

Safety Tips

Wear your goggles when your teacher tells you.

Handle materials carefully.

Never put things into your mouth.

Wash your hands after every activity.

Be kind to living things.

Always tell an adult
if you are hurt.

Clean up spills.

Using a
Hand Lens

A hand lens is a tool that makes objects look bigger. It helps you see the small parts of an object.

Look at a Coin

1. Place a coin on your desk.

2. Hold the hand lens above the coin. Look through the lens. Slowly move the lens away from the coin. What do you see?

3. Keep moving the lens away until the coin looks blurry.

4. Then slowly move the lens closer. Stop when the coin does not look blurry.

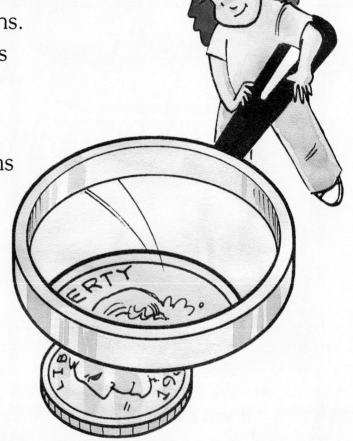

Using a
Thermometer

A thermometer is a tool used to measure temperature. Temperature tells how hot or cold something is. It is measured in degrees.

Find the Temperature of Water

1. Put water into a cup.

2. Put a thermometer into the cup.

3. Watch the colored liquid in the thermometer. What do you see?

4. Look how high the colored liquid is. What number is closest? That is the temperature of the water.

Using a
Ruler

A ruler is a tool used to measure the length of objects. Most rulers are 12 inches long. This length is called a foot.

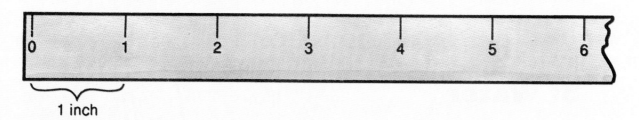

1 inch

Measure a Pencil

1. Place the ruler on your desk.

2. Lay your pencil next to the ruler. Line up one end with the 0 mark on the ruler.

3. Look at the other end of the pencil. Which number is closest to that end?

Using a
Calculator

A calculator is a tool that can help you add numbers. It can help you subtract numbers.

Subtract Numbers

1. Tim and Anna both grew plants.
Tim grew 8 plants.
Anna grew 17 plants.

2. How many more plants did Anna grow?
Use your calculator to find out.

3. Enter 17 on the calculator.
Then press the ⊖ key.
Enter **8** and press ⊜ .

4. What is your answer?

GLOSSARY

bacteria Tiny living things that can only be seen with a microscope. Some bacteria cause sickness. (E5)

beak The jaws of a bird along with their hard coverings. A bird uses its beak to pick up food. Beaks are also called bills. (A26)

beam A ray of light. A laser produces a narrow beam of light. (B18)

condense To change from a gas to a liquid. When water vapor in the air cools, it condenses to form clouds. (D35)

dinosaur An animal that lived millions of years ago. All dinosaurs lived on land. (C4)

endangered A living thing that may become extinct. The giant panda is an endangered animal. (C41)

erosion The washing away of the land. The roots of trees can help stop erosion. (A37)

evaporate To change from a liquid to a gas. Water evaporates to form water vapor. (D31)

extinct When all animals of one kind die. There are no dinosaurs today because these animals are extinct. (C40)

—— **F** ——

flat teeth Teeth that are good for grinding food. Many plant-eating dinosaurs had flat teeth. (C28)

fossil imprint A mark formed when a plant or animal leaves a trace, or print, of itself in soil, which gradually turns to rock. (C16)

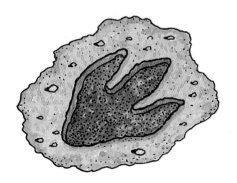

fossil remains What is left of a plant or animal that lived long ago. (C24)

fossil Remains or imprint of a once-living thing. Dinosaur footprints in rock are one kind of fossil. (C12)

freeze To change from a liquid to a solid. Water freezes into ice when the temperature is below 32°F. (D41)

—— **G** ——

gas A form of matter that does not have a set shape. A gas spreads out to fill what it is in. (D16)

germ A tiny living thing that can make you sick. (E4)

H

habitat A place in which a plant or animal lives. In its habitat a living thing gets all the things it needs. (A8)

heat A form of energy used to change matter. Heat is used to warm homes. Heat can change a solid to a liquid. (B14, D26)

I

injury Something harmful that happens to a person. Some injuries are cuts, scrapes, bruises, and broken bones. (E26)

L

leaves Parts of a plant that grow on a stem or grow up from roots. Leaves make food. (A13)

light A form of energy that you can see. The sun and the stars give off light. (B4)

liquid Matter that takes the shape of its container. (D8)

living thing Something that is alive. Living things move, need food, and grow. (A4)

lodge A beaver's home. (A32)

M

matter What all things are made of. All matter takes up space. (D4)

melt To change from a solid to a liquid. When ice melts, it changes to liquid water. (D40)

microscope A tool that makes small things appear larger. Bacteria can be seen with the aid of a microscope. (E4)

mucus A sticky material that traps germs and dust. It prevents these things from reaching the lungs. (E19)

nonliving thing Something that was never alive. A rock is a nonliving thing. (A5)

once-living thing Something that was alive at one time or was once part of a living thing. Logs used to make a fence are examples of once-living things. (A5)

opaque A material that keeps light from passing through. An opaque object casts a shadow. The human body and a paper bag are both opaque. (B22)

P

pointed teeth Sharp teeth that are good for tearing food. Many meat-eating dinosaurs had pointed teeth. (C28)

prevent To keep from happening. Wearing a helmet when skating can help prevent injury. (E27)

prism A clear object shaped like a pyramid. A prism bends light and separates it into the colors of the rainbow. (B39)

R

rainbow Made when drops of water in the sky act like prisms and break the sunlight into colors. The colors of the rainbow are red, orange, yellow, green, blue, indigo, and violet. (B38)

reflect To throw back. The moon reflects the light of the sun. (B11)

remains Fossils that were part of the real animal. Fossil bones are remains. (C12)

resource Anything that plants or animals use to live. (A19)

root The part of a plant that grows down into the soil. Roots hold the plant in place, soak up water, and sometimes store food. (A12)

S

shadow A dark shape formed when an object blocks light. Shadows can become longer or shorter. (B28)

shelter A place where an animal can rest and be safe. An animal stores food and raises its young in a shelter. (A22)

skeleton The bones of the body that hold up the body and help it move. Scientists have found dinosaur skeletons. (C34)

skull The bone that shapes your head and protects your brain. (C30)

sneeze A sudden forcing of breath through the nose and mouth. Sneezing is one way that germs are spread. (E8)

solid A form of matter that has its own shape. When a solid is put into a jar, the shape of the solid stays the same. (D4)

spine The tiny, sharp leaves of a cactus. Spines protect the plant from being eaten by animals. (A13)

spread To pass from one person to another. Diseases are spread by sneezing, coughing, and touching objects that have germs on them. (E13)

stem The supporting and connecting part of a plant. Water and food move through stems. (A12)

straight Not bent or curved. Light travels in a straight line. (B19)

texture The way something feels. Rough and smooth are textures. (D5)

translucent Allowing some light to pass through. Some translucent objects are frosted glass and waxed paper. (B22)

transparent Allowing light to pass through. Clear water and plastic wrap are transparent. (B22)

V
---

virus A very small germ that causes sickness. Viruses are too small to be seen with most microscopes. (E5)

W
---

water cycle The changes that happen to water in nature. The steps of the water cycle are (1) water evaporates, (2) water condenses to form clouds, (3) water falls as rain, (4) water evaporates again. (D37)

water vapor Water that is a gas. You cannot see water vapor. (D31)

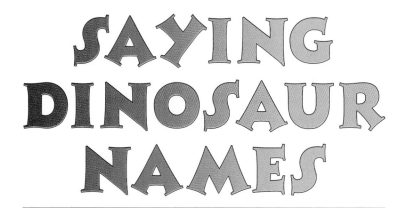

SAYING DINOSAUR NAMES

Albertosaurus al bur tuh SAWR us

Allosaurus al oh SAWR us

Ankylosaurus ang kuh loh SAWR us

Brachiosaurus brak *ee* uh SAWR us

Compsognathus kahmp SAHG nuh thus

Corythosaurus kawr ihnth uh SAWR us

Diplodocus dih PLAHD uh kus

Edmontosaurus ed mahn tuh SAWR us

Lambeosaurus lam bee oh SAWR us

Ornitholestes awr nih thuh LES teez

Ouranosaurus uh rahn uh SAWR us

Seismosaurus syz muh SAWR us

Stenonychosaurus sten oh nyk uh SAWR us

Triceratops trye SER uh tahps

Tyrannosaurus tuh ran uh SAWR us

Velociraptor vuh LAHS uh rap tur

INDEX

T

teeth
of dinosaurs, C28–C31
flat, C28
pointed, C28
texture, D5
translucent, B22–B25
transparent, B22–B25

V

virus, E5

W

water cycle, D37
water vapor, D31, D34

CREDITS

Cover: *Photography:* Jade Albert; *Photography Production:* Picture It Corporation; *Illustration:* Doreen Gay-Kassel.

ILLUSTRATORS
UNIT A A14–A15: Robert Roper. **A22–A23:** Debbie Pinkney Davis. **A30–A33:** Bob Pepper. **A36–A37:** Jenny Campbell. **A46:** Tom Pansini.

UNIT B B4–B5: Katie Keller. **B8–B11:** Ron Young. **B14–B15:** Jackie Urbanovic. **B28–B31:** Peggy Tagel. **B42–B45:** Eugenie Fernandes. **B46:** Tom Pansini.

UNIT C C4–C5: Richard Courtney. **C8–C9:** Phil Wilson. **C20–C21:** *t.* Taylor Oughton; *b.* Ka Botzis. **C24–C25:** Mike Meaker. **C28–C31:** Phil Wilson. **C36–C37:** Phil Wilson. **C42:** Tom Pansini.

UNIT D D36–D37: Carolyn Croll. **D44–D45:** Brian Karas. **D46:** Tom Pansini.

UNIT E E22–E23: Doreen Gay-Kassel. **E24–E25:** Eldon Doty. **E26–E27:** Jerry Zimmerman. **E30–E31:** Jenny Campbell. **E32–E33:** Tom Pansini.

GLOSSARY: Tom Pansini.

PHOTOGRAPHS
All photographs by Silver Burdett Ginn (SBG) unless otherwise noted.

UNIT A A4–A5: Randy Wells/Allstock/Tony Stone Images. **A8:** Laurence Hughes/The Image Bank. **A9:** Pat O'Hara/Allstock/Tony Stone Images. **A12–A15:** Runk/Schoenberger/Grant Heilman Photography. **A18–A19:** James Randklev/Allstock/Tony Stone Images. **A26–A27:** *t.l.* © Francis Gohier/Photo Researchers, Inc.; *t.m.* William J. Weber/Visuals Unlimited; *t.r.* Darrell Gulin/Allstock/Tony Stone Images; *b.l., b.r.* ZEFA Germany/The Stock Market; *b.m.* Tom Tietz/Tony Stone Images. **A30, A32:** *t.l.* © Pat & Tom Leeson/Photo Researchers, Inc.; *m.l.* Tom Mangelson/Images of Nature; *b.l.* Johnny Johnson/Animals Animals. **A40–A41:** Gabe Palmer/The Stock Market. **A44:** Tony Stone Images. **A45:** Charles Kreb/Allstock. **A47:** Erwin & Peggy Bauer/Bruce Coleman, Inc.

UNIT B B18–B19: Peter Fox for SBG. **B22–B25:** Superstock. **B34–B35:** Peter Fox for SBG. **B38–B39:** G. Nagele/FPG International.

UNIT C C12: Courtesy, Peter Gregg. **C12–C13:** Jim Richardson/Westlight. **C16:** Breck P. Kent. **C16–C17:** Tom Bean. **C34–C37:** Mike Peters for SBG. **C40–C41:** Frans Lanting/Minden Pictures. **C43:** Louis Psihoyos/Matrix International, Inc.

UNIT D D16: *t.l.* B. Taylor/H. Armstrong Roberts; *m.l.* Tony Freeman/PhotoEdit; *b.l.* Michael Newman/PhotoEdit. **D16–D17:** Shelly Boyd/PhotoEdit. **D30–D31:** Tom McCarthy/PhotoEdit. **D34–D37:** Martin Rogers/Stock Boston. **D40–D41:** Oz Charles.

UNIT E E4: *t.* © Michael Abbey/Photo Researchers, Inc; *b.* © Biophoto Associates/Science Source/Photo Researchers, Inc. **E5:** *t.* © CNRI/Science Photo Library/Photo Researchers, Inc; *b.* © CDC/Science Source/Photo Researchers, Inc. **E8–E9:** Globus Studios for SBG. **E9:** © P. Hawtin, University of Southampton/Science Photo Library/Photo Researchers, Inc. **E14:** © David Phillips/Photo Researchers, Inc. **E14–E15:** © CNRI/Science Photo Library/Photo Researchers, Inc. **E15:** © NIBSC/Science Photo Library/Photo Researchers, Inc. **E18–E19:** David Phillips. **E22–E23:** Grant Huntington for SBG.